Mother

An Illustrated Tribute

by Aubrey Bjork

Petrichor Press
ISBN 9798654835413

Contents

Introduction

I wasn't planning on becoming a mother. I wasn't even planning on becoming a wife. I wasn't interested in babies or nap times, or kindergarten through twelfth grade. The thought of having my own children brought a lump to my throat.

It has been a process, learning to love the hike called motherhood. Many times I've curled up on the floor and cried, worn out by the the weight of carrying and caring for another human life. My children's tears have mingled with my own as I've wept over my weaknesses and deficiencies.

But being a mother, as I've discovered, is finding strength in weakness. Instead of staying on the floor amidst the scattered Laffy Taffy wrappers, I choose in, as my mothers chose before me.

I choose to rise.

I choose to love.

I choose to lift.

I am so grateful for the mothers along the way who have showed me the dignity and beauty of motherhood. Not just in scrubbing floors, wiping noses, and juggling schedules. Not just in cooking (or burning) daily meals or changing flat tires. Not in the — well, you get the idea. The to-do list sits on my chest and wags its finger in my face.

Until I let it go. Then, like my mothers before me, I help to rescue Princess Lilystar from the dread clutches of her unamed (and often lovingly armless) nemesis. I read just one more story, even though we've read *Hello, Ninja* 15 times this week already. I choose to show up.

Don't get me wrong. The Lord asked us to strengthen the feeble knees for a reason. All too often mine crumple under the mountain of last straws: sippy cups with crooked lids, an unidentifiable sploosh on the kitchen floor, or another drink in the middle of the night. My heart breaks over tough questions and even tougher answers.

Sometimes, even with great examples, support, and resources, I still need to rest.

In those moments, a line from my mothers echoes in my heart.

"When care is pressing you down a bit /

rest if you must, but don't you quit."

I am deeply comforted by, and — as I mentioned before — deeply grateful for the women who have invited me to instill the wayposts of wisdom in my heart that keep me going day to day, hour to hour, minute to minute.

I know they—like me—have made mistakes. They're not perfect, and ached from their own inadequacies and imperfections.

Maybe that's why they're so beautiful to me. Not because they were perfectly polished people— but because they weren't, and yet they chose in, anyway.

Hopefully this small compendium gives just a taste of what it feels like to be a mother—and how worth it, how valuable it is to be one.

To continue in the words of John Greenleaf Whittier,

"So stick to the fight when you're hardest hit—It's when things seem worst that you must not quit."

Aubrey Bjork

I LOVE
YOU

Minutes

Last minute panic
comes at eleven, of course
in trips to the store.

A dress made from rags
the minutes pieced together
and perfectly suit.

One minute later
cakes benches beds walls floors sink
appear from nowhere.

The creation drive
that shapes the vibrant soul in
the work of minutes.

The Skunk

One day my young son wanted
to paint an old, dead stump.
I wrapped him in an apron,
from the brush smoothed out the clumps.

Soon sister, too, asked for a brush
to paint upon that tree
I sent her out with her own brush,
as happy as a breeze.

Not two minutes later
Not even quite a wink
returned two paint-stained children
in need of washing at the sink.

Amidst the explanation
of paint not quite on log,
I found out to my horror
that paint had got on dog.

So if by chance you're wondering
why it is we own a skunk
that white stripe upon her back
was meant for that dead trunk.

There

Your hands welcomed them
The first cries echoed
in your ears
in your heart
and hope was born.

It wasn't always easy
the long days
the long nights
the empty hours and frantic minutes.
But you know that.
You were there.

The first steps
The first words
Halting steps
Stammered words
were yours and theirs to share.
Broken toys
Broken hearts
passed under your care.

Was it enough?
No.
But you were.

You made mistakes
things you didn't say,
things you did.
But
More importantly
you made moments.

Birthday cakes
Opportunites
Space in your heart
Space in your arms

One sacrifice set on another
built a house of love.

It might seem empty
the bricks worn and faded.
But the smell of those bricks
the smell of love
there
will always guide them home.

Little Bird

Some souls are beautiful
gentle
unearthly
Like the song of the little bird
who reminds us
what the song of our souls
sounds like.

Grandma

A is for apples
neatly cut in half.
B is for backyard
the place where children laugh.
C is for Christmas
with a glorious green tree.
D is for the dog
who someone named Murphy.
E is for excitment
when we walk in the door.
F is for forgetting
the toys left on the floor.
G is for gone,
out fishing, biking, too.
H is for help,
a shepherd at the zoo.
I is for imagination,
sailing down the nile.
J is for a funny joke
that passes 'round the smiles.

K is for camping,
at least it sounds that way.
L is for Lilliput,
a friend in child's play.
M is for meals,
Lord bless you for them all.
N is for need,
you've been there, big and small.
O is for the outdoors,
red rock, mountains, lakes.
P is for the daily prayers
you offer for our sakes.
Q is for the royal Queen,
with spatula as scepter.
R is for the rest we find
when we spend time together.
S is for the stories,
that echo from the past.
T is for the time you've spent,
making memories last.

U is for the underwear
you've rinsed and cleaned and washed.
V is for the vomit
Well—that's best forgot.
W is for the weeks
we spent under your care.
X marks the hidden spot
there's buried fruit snacks there.
Y is for the years to come
fulfilled, with love and peace.
Z is for the gentle snore,
of happy kids at rest.

In a moment she looked directly at him and there was
a sharp lift to her tone. "I know when I'm well off, Troy.
I ain't changin' nothin', ain't allowin' nothin' to happen
that could change anything. Yes, dammit, I love Tom."
Troy smoked and watched her with that thin veil of laz
amusement. When her talk had ended, he shrugged
shoulders elaborately, flicked the ash down at his side
was just askin'," he said calmly. "Wasn't no need t

Your Words

It was your voice
your words
drifting over the back of the couch
floating through the mayhem
that first opened the world.

It was your words
your voice
that spoke of broken monsters
wounded pride
and sour grapes.

It was your voice
your words
patiently
slowly
that opened up a world.

It Seems

I don't mean to probe or doubt
but it seems to be,
the making of the perfect smore
might be the death of me.

Gaps

Somehow the pizza
creeps into every corner.
Cowboy
Artichoke
Feta Cheese
The harbingers of peace
and harmony.
It falls through the cracks,
filling up the gaps
I didn't know were aching.

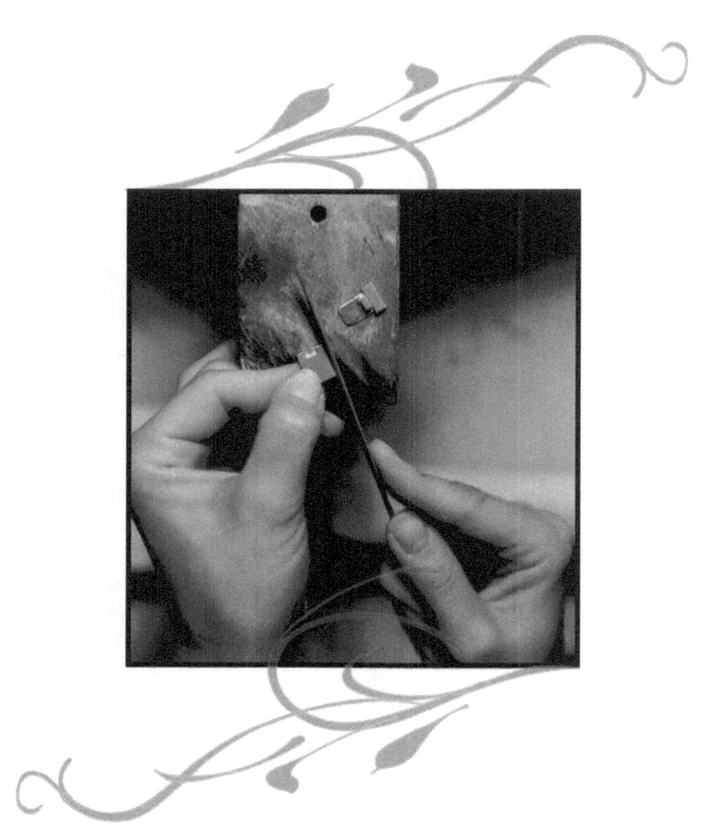

Fire

Some men are only found in fire,
and tempered by the heat.
Each scorch, each scar, each burning brand
the byways guide their feet.

And midst the ash and smoke appears
a heart wreathed in blue flame.
The arms and hands now speak the truth
of valor made through pain.

A Word

If I could put you in a word,
I don't know what I'd choose.
Thing finder, quick helper,
a gem too good to lose.

You're the song stuck in my head,
the peace of work well done.
La la la, strokes up and down
the colors blend and run.

You're the assassin bound in silence,
private as an eye,
but there inside, when I catch a peep,
you're shining, deep and bright.